Be like a *Beautiful Butterfly*
and enjoy life's many changes

MONA'S MISSION

The Story of Monarch Migration

ELLEN DALZELL
ILLUSTRATED BY PENNY BROWN

◆ FriesenPress

One Printers Way
Altona, MB R0G 0B0
Canada

www.friesenpress.com

Copyright © 2023 Ellen Dalzell
First Edition — 2023

All rights reserved.

No part of this publication may be reproduced in any form, or by any means, electronic or mechanical, including photocopying, recording, or any information browsing, storage, or retrieval system, without permission in writing from FriesenPress.

Illustrated by Penny Brown.

ISBN
978-1-03-917759-8 (Hardcover)
978-1-03-917758-1 (Paperback)
978-1-03-917760-4 (eBook)

1. JUVENILE NONFICTION, ANIMALS, BUTTERFLIES, MOTHS & CATERPILLARS

Distributed to the trade by The Ingram Book Company

Dedication

MONA'S MISSION is dedicated to all friends and family who have encouraged me once again to write a book which shares my love for nature in our world. Thank you to those who purchased my first book, *The Missing Toe*. Its success led me to put pen to paper and create my second book, *Mona's Mission*.

I am blessed to have a wonderful friend with outstanding artistic talent. Penny Brown, my illustrator, took a good book and changed it into a work of art. Thank you, Penny, for once again using your art to enhance my book.

I would also like to thank my friend, Austin Davis, for guiding me through all of the technology required to complete the publishing of this book. I couldn't have done it without your help.

Mona is a third-generation female monarch butterfly. The previous two generations left the states of Michigan, Minnesota, or Wisconsin to spend their short two-to-six-week lives traveling southward on the monarch migration to Mexico. After emerging from her chrysalis in July of 2022, Mona's mission begins. She will spend her six-week lifespan mating, laying eggs, consuming nectar from pollinating plants, and sleeping in tall treetops. Let's join Mona on her six-week journey as she fulfills her mission.

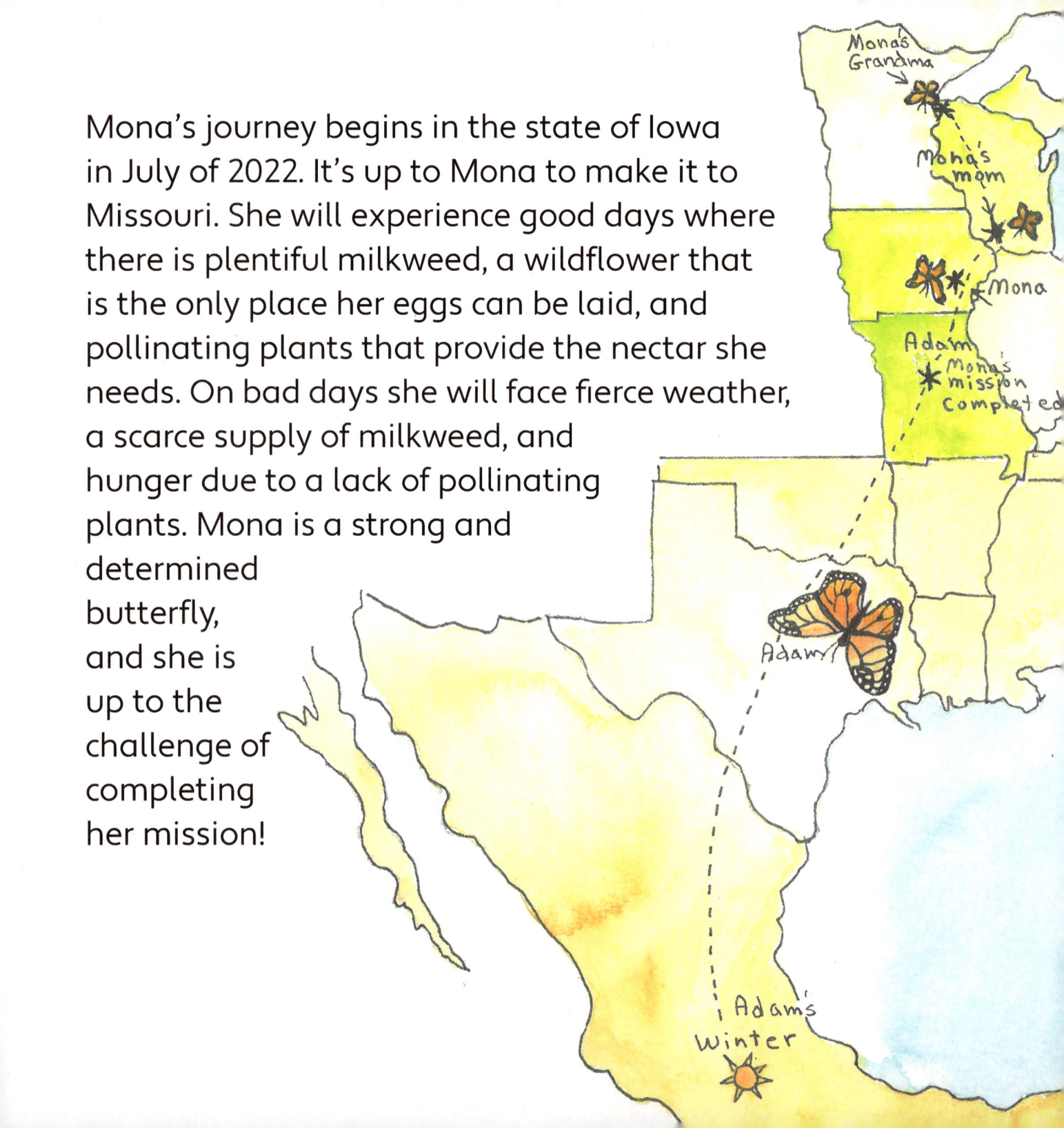

Mona's journey begins in the state of Iowa in July of 2022. It's up to Mona to make it to Missouri. She will experience good days where there is plentiful milkweed, a wildflower that is the only place her eggs can be laid, and pollinating plants that provide the nectar she needs. On bad days she will face fierce weather, a scarce supply of milkweed, and hunger due to a lack of pollinating plants. Mona is a strong and determined butterfly, and she is up to the challenge of completing her mission!

Monarch butterflies like Mona can cover from fifty to one hundred miles on a good day. She is very excited to begin her journey, but first her wings must lengthen and dry. When that happens, Mona soars up into the branches of a tall tree where she will rest for a short time. The underside of big leaves on the tree provide protection from bad weather and butterfly predators while she sleeps.

Mona's first day of life is spent resting her wings to gain strength and consuming nectar to give her energy. She will need lots of strength and energy to complete her mission. She has many miles to cover during her short six-week life, but Mona is a determined lady!

When she is well-rested, Mona will use her sense of smell to find her food, the nectar from pollinating plants. Her proboscis is used to suck the nectar from the flowers. She spends the day flitting from flower to flower, finding nourishment from coneflowers, bee balm, asters, black-eyed Susans, and sedum. She is grateful to the gardeners who plant milkweed and these butterfly-friendly flowers.

When the sun sets and the air cools, Mona searches for a treetop where she can roost with other migrating monarchs. A lot of wing flapping occurs as more and more monarchs enter the tree for a good night's rest. Wing flapping is the way butterflies communicate with each other. Mona is happy to have company. She is a "social butterfly"!

A new day dawns, and when the sun warms the air, Mona and her friends fly from the protection of the treetop and begin their day soaring above farm fields, towns, and cities as they travel southward. After about ten hours of flying, Mona begins searching for a patch of milkweed where she can lay her eggs. Remember, female monarchs use only milkweed leaves for their egglaying. Mona is happy that more and more people are planting milkweed to make her journey easier.

Most of Mona's days are spent flying, laying eggs, consuming nectar, and resting in treetops. These days take her through Iowa and into the state of Missouri. She shows courage, strength, and endurance as she works hard to complete her mission. We wonder... how can something so small be so strong?

On some days, Mona is unable to fly southward due to bad weather. Strong winds and rain force her to remain sheltered in the protective thickness of treetops. When the storms pass, she searches for food and then continues her journey.

Mona is very happy that people are providing milkweed and pollinating plants along her migration path. Her vision is not very good, so she relies on her strong sense of smell to guide her to these plants. Her survival depends on these plants. When she lays her eggs on milkweed, they hatch into caterpillars which soon become chrysalises. From the chrysalises emerge beautiful monarch butterflies that will complete the journey to Mexico when Mona's life is over.

There are many dangers for Mona as she completes her part of the monarch migration. Birds, snakes, and lizards are just a few of her treetop enemies. Closer to the ground she must be on the lookout for such things as cats, praying mantises, wasps, spiders, and frogs. When flying across highways, she needs to avoid the windshields of trucks and cars.

After five weeks of migrating, Mona makes it to the middle of Missouri. She is delighted to find clear skies, big farm fields with scattered patches of milkweed, big cities, and lots of small towns. She looks for a nice little town with everything she needs to make her last week of life very pleasant.

Knowing her time is short, Mona decides to lay her final eggs in a pretty little garden beside a beautiful historic library in the small town of Glasgow, Missouri. The garden has milkweed, pollinating plants, and benches for people to sit and enjoy the sights and sounds of nature. Mona knows this is the perfect place for her mission to end.

In the garden, Mona locates a fresh milkweed plant for her eggs. Once she has deposited her eggs, she enjoys a final meal of nectar from the nice-smelling flowers. Mona no longer has the strength to fly to the treetops so she lies down in the grass beside the garden. As she slowly passes away, she is happy knowing her mission is now complete. In her six weeks, she has produced many eggs. These eggs will hatch and create the super generation that will complete
the journey to Mexico.
Congratulations Mona!
Your mission is complete.

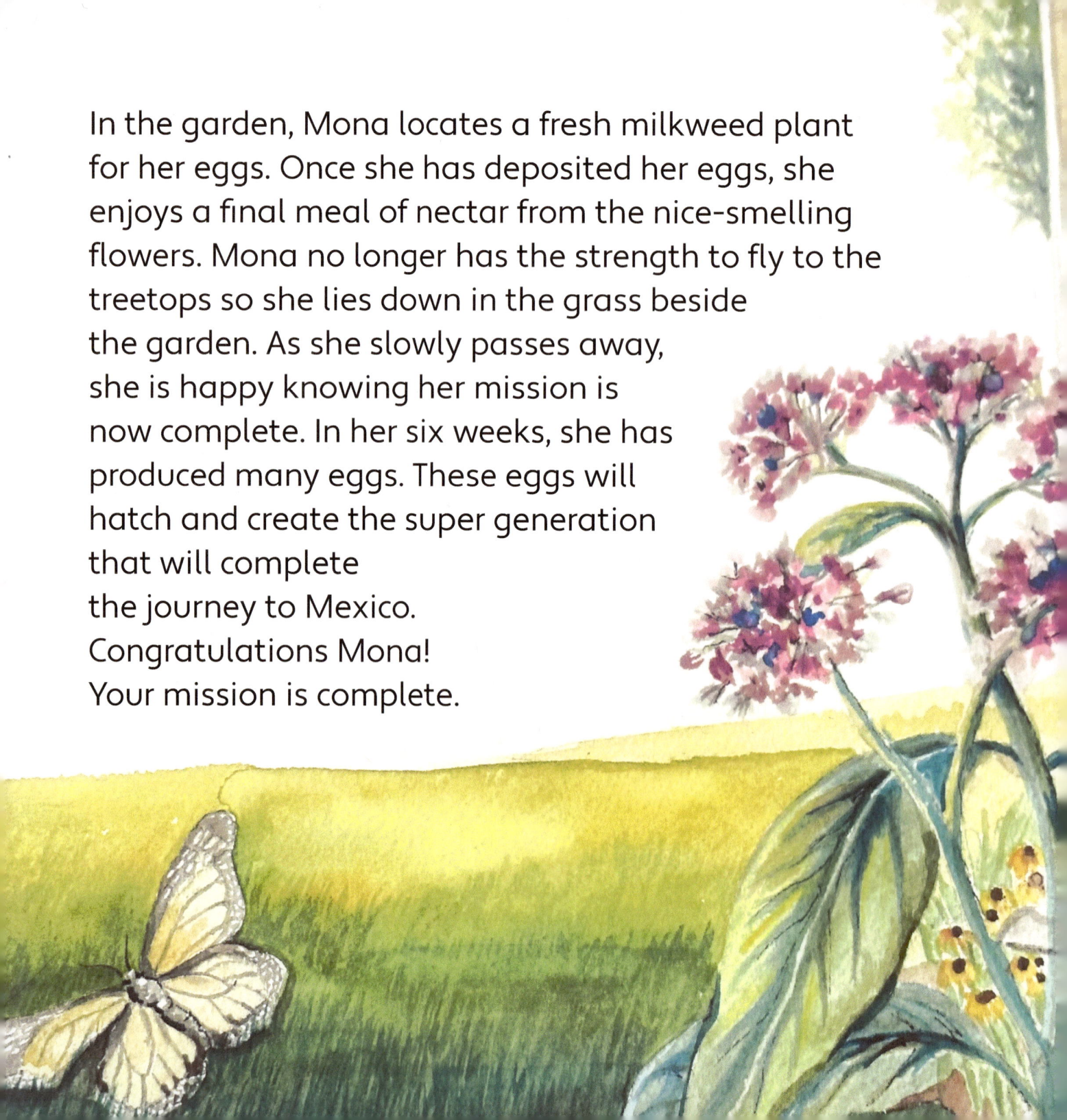

After the passing of Mona, the garden caretaker finds a big, beautiful caterpillar happily chewing milkweed leaves in the garden. She takes care of it until he or she becomes a super generation monarch butterfly. After about two weeks, a handsome male monarch emerges! The caretaker decides to name him Adam because he is the first male in the Glasgow Butterfly Garden. Once his wings strengthen, Adam is on his way, completing Mona's mission.
VAYA CON DIOS, ADAM!

Several weeks after all the monarchs have left Missouri on their way to Mexico, a nice, talented young man creates a wooden carving of Mona and donates it to the Glasgow Butterfly Garden. Thanks to his gift, Mona will always be remembered by those who visit this special garden.

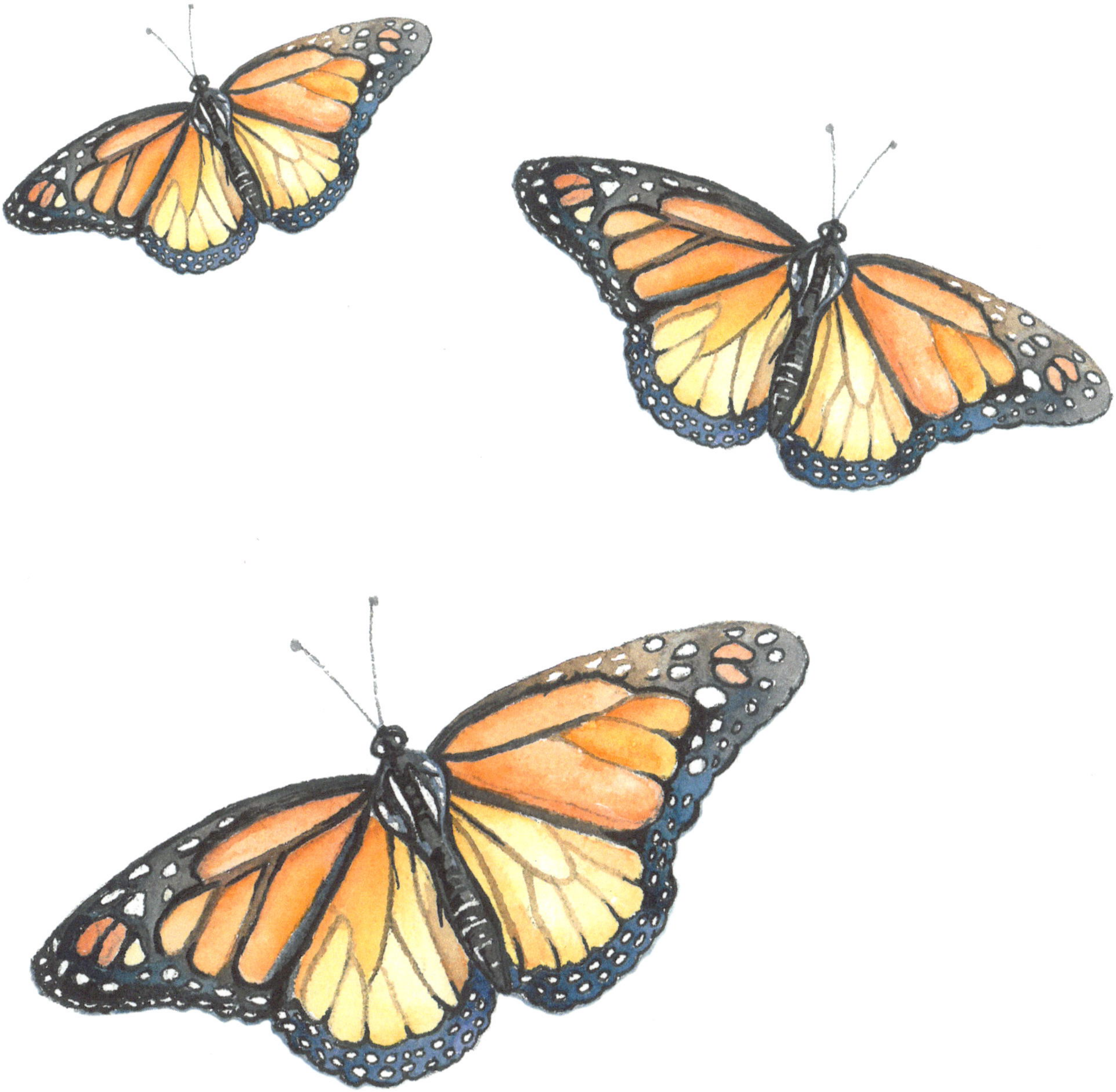

Monarch butterflies like Mona are expert travelers. In the late spring of each year, they leave their homes in southern Canada, Minnesota, Michigan, and Wisconsin. Their journey southward to Mexico is very similar to a relay race. Those beginning the race are the first generation. They have a life span of about six weeks. The second and third generations follow the first generation, flying many miles, consuming nectar from pollinating plants, and laying eggs. Their life span is the same as the first generation. Mona is a part of the third generation. It is her job to fly as far as possible and lay eggs that will become the fourth generation, which is known as the "super generation." They have a life span of eight to nine months, and it is their job to finish the journey to their winter home in Mexico. They roost in special evergreen trees in a mountainous part of Mexico.

When spring arrives, they wake up, search for nectar, lay eggs, and then pass away. The eggs hatch into caterpillars which then become chrysalises and emerge into beautiful butterflies. It is their mission during their six weeks of life to fly back to their home in the north.

What amazing creatures these monarch butterflies are! Not only are they beautiful, they play an important role in pollination, which is required for our food supply. Let's do whatever we can to ensure their survival by planting milkweed and pollinating plants.

Ingram Content Group UK Ltd.
Milton Keynes UK
UKHW050426060623
422931UK00004B/43